Italian Salads

Italian Salads

Maxine Clark photography by Diana Miller

RYLAND
PETERS
& SMALL
LONDON NEW YORK

First published in Great Britain in 2006
by Ryland Peters & Small
20–21 Jockey's Fields
London WC1R 4BW
www.rylandpeters.com

10 9 8 7 6 5 4 3 2 1

ISBN-13: 978 1 84597 133 5
ISBN-10: 1 84597 133 7

A CIP record for this book is available
from the British Library.

Printed in China

Notes

• All spoon measurements are level unless
otherwise specified.
• All eggs are medium unless otherwise
specified. Uncooked or partly cooked eggs
should not be served to the very young,
the frail or elderly, those with compromised
immune systems or to pregnant women.

Acknowledgments

Thanks to Elsa for commissioning me to write
about a subject close to our hearts! At last
I have worked with the lovely Diana Miller
who took such care over the photography
and became a friend. Antonia found the
most stunning props to complement the
food and photography. Thanks also go to
Megan for her beautiful design and to
Sharon, my long-suffering, understanding
and very exacting editor. Special thanks go
to Lizzie Harris, who helped me out at the
studio when it all got too much!

Senior Designer Megan Smith
Commissioning Editor
    Elsa Petersen-Schepelern
Editor Sharon Cochrane
Production Paul Harding
Art Director Anne-Marie Bulat
Editorial Director Julia Charles
Publishing Director Alison Starling

Food Stylist Maxine Clark
Stylist Antonia Gaunt
Index Hilary Bird

Contents

Salads Italian-style 6

Fast & Fresh 8

Cooked Vegetables 22

Fish & Seafood 42

Meat 56

Index 64

Salads
Italian-style

Salads are an important part of the Italian way of life.

They aid the digestion and clear the palate and often take the place of a vegetable side dish or *contorno*. The ingredients are always fresh and dressed very simply with oil, vinegar, salt and pepper. In the south of Italy, the vinegar may be replaced by freshly squeezed lemon juice.

On my travels I have come across many types of salads, from light and delicate mixtures of spring leaves to hot salads made with potato mixed with salame in a warm dressing. There are countless variations and they all depend on what is in season. A typical winter salad at Christmas will contain crisp cauliflower mixed with colourful peppers and a hint of rich anchovy. Summer salads will be green and crisp with seasonal sweet or bitter leaves. Some salads are cooked, then served cold on a large platter as a family feast. There is something for everyone.

The important thing to remember is that the salad should not be drowned or overpowered by a dressing. To dress a salad the Italian way, basic condiments such as oil, vinegar, salt and pepper are usually provided at the table so you can dress your own. When dressing a salad, add a good pinch of salt to the salad in the bowl, sprinkle in a little vinegar, swoosh a stream of extra virgin olive oil in a circular movement over the whole lot, grind over some freshly ground black pepper and toss really well before serving. Otherwise, put one part vinegar or freshly squeezed lemon juice in the bottom of a bowl. Sprinkle in some salt and mix to dissolve, then whisk in four parts oil and some freshly ground black pepper. Add the salad and toss gently with clean hands or salad servers until evenly coated with the dressing. Transfer the salad to a clean serving bowl and serve immediately.

Italian salads always start with good, fresh, seasonal ingredients. Choose the mixture of ingredients carefully, planning contrasts of flavours and textures, and don't add too many – the simpler the better. Some crisp cos lettuce with a drop of lemon juice and olive oil can be divine!

Fast & Fresh

Insalata Caprese, this classic salad born on the Isle of Capri, is hard to beat. It combines three ingredients that work totally in harmony with each other. The first is mozzarella, preferably soft, creamy *mozzarella di bufala*. Tomato – this must be red and ripe, and the same size as the ball of mozzarella – and basil, which must be fresh, pungent and plentiful. Although not strictly Italian, sliced avocado is a delicious addition. To make this salad really sing of sunny Capri, use the best possible ingredients and be generous with them. Personally, I don't use vinegar to dress this salad as I think it can spoil the delicate flavours.

Tomato, Mozzarella and Basil Salad

2 balls of buffalo mozzarella, 150 g each

2 large ripe tomatoes, roughly the same size as the balls of mozzarella

50 g fresh basil leaves

about 100 ml extra virgin olive oil

sea salt and freshly ground black pepper

Serves 4

Cut the mozzarella and tomatoes into slices about 5 mm thick. Arrange the tomato slices on a large plate and season with salt and pepper. Put 1 slice of mozzarella on each slice of tomato and top with a basil leaf. Tear up the remaining basil and scatter over the top. Drizzle with a generous amount of olive oil just before serving.

This salad must be made at the last moment to prevent the tomatoes from weeping and the mozzarella from drying out. Serve at room temperature, never chilled, as this would kill the flavours.

Variation If using avocado, halve and peel one ripe avocado, remove the stone and slice the flesh. Intersperse the slices of avocado with the tomato and mozzarella.

You might not think this dish is very Italian, but it originates from the Alto Adige region in northern Italy near Austria, where cucumbers and soured cream are very popular. It is a legacy from the old Austro-Hungarian empire. It is particularly delicious served alongside cold chicken or poached salmon.

Grated Cucumber, Soured Cream and Paprika Salad

2 large cucumbers

a bunch of spring onions, trimmed and very finely shredded or 1 small red onion, very finely chopped

2 teaspoons tarragon vinegar

6 tablespoons soured cream

2 teaspoons sweet paprika

sea salt and freshly ground black pepper

Serves 4

Wash the cucumbers in warm soapy water to remove any wax or residues. Rinse and dry well. Grate them on the rough side of a cheese grater – it shouldn't be too fine. Transfer to a sieve or colander set over a plate, sprinkle with salt and mix well. Let drain for 30 minutes.

Rinse the grated cucumber under cold running water, pat dry with a clean tea towel, then transfer to a bowl. Add the onions and vinegar and mix with a fork. Season well with salt and pepper. Spread the cucumber mixture in an even layer on a serving plate.

Season the soured cream with salt, pepper and a pinch of paprika, then spoon it over the top of the cucumber mixture. Sprinkle liberally with the remaining paprika and serve immediately.

Tomato, Cucumber and Onion Salad

4 medium ripe tomatoes, or
20 cherry tomatoes

1 large cucumber

1 medium red onion

4 tablespoons extra virgin olive oil

1 tablespoon red wine vinegar

$1/2$ teaspoon chilli flakes

1 tablespoon chopped
fresh oregano

sea salt and freshly ground
black pepper

Serves 4

A robust salad to be made when tomatoes are at their best. You could add some black olives and cubed salted ricotta to make this a more substantial Greco-Italian salad.

Quarter the large tomatoes or halve the cherry tomatoes. Cut the cucumber into even-sized chunks about the same size as the tomatoes. Slice the red onion into thin rings.

Put the oil, vinegar, chilli flakes, oregano and salt and pepper to taste in a bowl and whisk well. Add the onion and toss to coat. Set aside for 10 minutes for the onion to soften. Add the tomato and cucumber to the onion, mix gently and serve immediately.

Simple Mixed Leaf Salad

1 medium lettuce, leaves
separated, or 4 handfuls
mixed salad leaves

freshly squeezed lemon juice

extra virgin olive oil, in an olive
oil pourer/decanter

sea salt and freshly ground
black pepper

Serves 4

When eating out in Italy, the condiments to dress your salad – normally olive oil, wine vinegar, salt and pepper – are usually provided separately so you can dress it to your liking.

Wash the salad leaves and dry well in a salad spinner or with a clean tea towel. Put in a salad bowl and sprinkle with a good pinch of salt. Sprinkle in a few drops of lemon juice, followed by a generous swirling flourish of olive oil. Grind over plenty of black pepper and toss lightly but thoroughly. Serve immediately, adding more lemon juice, oil, salt or pepper to taste at the table.

The combination of young emerald-green broad beans and nutty pecorino is the essence of spring in Tuscany. Pecorino, a ewe's milk cheese, is delightful served with a drizzle of local honey, so I have incorporated it into a dressing for this salad. Don't be tempted to add anything else to the salad – it is just perfect as it is. When broad beans aren't in season, use raw fresh young peas instead. This makes a delicious starter.

Broad Beans and Pecorino with Honey and Lemon Dressing

1 kg fresh young broad beans in the pod (400 g podded weight)

250 g young pecorino cheese (pecorino toscano, if possible)

6 tablespoons extra virgin olive oil

2 tablespoons freshly squeezed lemon juice

1 tablespoon light and fragrant clear honey, such as acacia

sea salt and freshly ground black pepper

crusty bread, to serve (optional)

Serves 4–6

Remove the broad beans from their pods. If they are very young, you don't need to peel each individual bean. However, if they are larger and the skins are tough, you may have to peel them. To do this, plunge them into a saucepan of boiling water for 1 minute, drain and refresh in cold water. Pop them out of their grey skins, revealing the bright green bean inside. Transfer to a bowl.

Trim any rind from the pecorino and cut the cheese into cubes, about the same size as the biggest bean, and add to the beans.

Put the oil, lemon juice, honey, salt and pepper in a bowl and whisk. Pour over the salad, toss gently to mix and serve immediately with crusty bread, if using.

This is one of the most refreshing salads for a hot summer's day. Antonella, my Tuscan friend who occasionally helps me in the kitchen, makes the best *panzanella*, as this salad is known. Hers is as light as air and not at all stodgy. Her secret is her light hands – like pastry making, overworking the bread will make it slimy. The bread soaks up the juices from the vegetables and the olive oil and is sharpened by the touch of vinegar. Mix the basil in at the last moment to prevent it from turning black.

Tuscan Bread and Summer Vegetable Salad

2 thick slices of stale white country bread (Tuscan saltless is best), at least 1 day old

4 large very ripe tomatoes, deseeded and diced

1 small red onion, finely chopped

1/2 cucumber, diced

1 small celery stick, diced

1 garlic clove, crushed

2 tablespoons red wine vinegar

6 tablespoons extra virgin olive oil

20 g fresh basil leaves, roughly torn, plus extra to serve

sea salt and freshly ground black pepper

Serves 4

Cut off the crusts from the bread and discard them. Tear the bread into small pieces and put in a bowl. Sprinkle with 1–2 tablespoons cold water – the bread should be only just moist, not soggy. Work the bread with your fingers – like rubbing in butter when making pastry – to distribute the moisture through the bread and break it into smaller crumbs.

Add the tomatoes, onion, cucumber, celery and garlic to the bread and mix lightly. Drizzle with the vinegar, half the olive oil and season well with salt and pepper. Toss very gently. Cover and let stand for 30 minutes so the bread absorbs the flavours.

Lightly mix in the torn basil, then serve drizzled with the remaining olive oil and scattered with extra basil leaves.

Orange and Bitter Leaf Salad
with Tomato and Olive Dressing

2 large oranges

200 g bitter leaves, such as escarole, frisée, chicory or a mixture

about 1 tablespoon pomegranate seeds (optional)

tomato and olive dressing

finely grated zest and juice of 1 unwaxed orange

6 tablespoons extra virgin olive oil

2 tablespoons finely shredded fresh basil leaves

2 tablespoons finely chopped, stoned, Greek-style black olives

4 sun-dried tomatoes in oil, drained and finely chopped

sea salt and freshly ground black pepper

Serves 4

This is a heavenly salad on a blistering hot day. Keep everything except the dressing in the fridge and assemble right at the last moment for maximum crispness. Make the dressing well in advance to allow the flavours to develop. You must use a bitter leaf here – the dressing and oranges will sweeten it. Pomegranate seeds add crunch and colour to this simple salad.

To make the tomato and olive dressing, put the orange zest and juice, olive oil, basil, olives and sun-dried tomatoes in a bowl and mix well. Season to taste with salt and pepper, cover and set aside to develop the flavours.

Using a sharp knife, peel the oranges and remove the white pith. Cut out the segments or slice them very thinly. Set aside.

Wash the bitter leaves and dry well in a salad spinner or with a clean tea towel. Tear into large pieces. Arrange in a serving bowl and tuck the orange segments or slices around them. Spoon over the dressing and scatter with the pomegranate seeds, if using. Serve immediately.

Lemon juice really brings out the flavour of raw mushrooms – add a little at first, then taste the dressing and add more if it needs it. When they are in season, this is best made with fresh wild mushrooms such as porcini. If these aren't available, use the best and tastiest mushrooms you can find. Button mushrooms just won't do – they have no flavour. Sometimes I add a dash of balsamic vinegar as it goes so well with mushrooms.

Mushroom and Rocket Salad
with Lemon Dressing

350 g mushrooms, preferably wild mushrooms such as porcini

finely grated zest and juice of 1 unwaxed lemon

6 tablespoons olive oil, plus extra for drizzling

200 g rocket, young spinach or watercress

50 g Parmesan cheese

2 tablespoons finely chopped fresh oregano

sea salt and freshly ground black pepper

Serves 4

Wipe the mushrooms, slice them thinly and put in a bowl.

Put the lemon zest, olive oil and lemon juice, to taste, in a small bowl and whisk. Season well with salt and pepper. Pour over the mushrooms and toss gently to coat evenly. Let marinate for at least 10 minutes so the mushrooms absorb the dressing.

When ready to serve, arrange the rocket, spinach or watercress on a large plate or in 4 individual bowls. Drizzle with olive oil and season with salt and pepper. Pile the mushrooms on top, leaving a fringe of greenery around the edges.

Using a vegetable peeler, shave thin strips of Parmesan over the mushrooms, then sprinkle with oregano and serve.

Cooked Vegetables

The potatoes absorb the glorious golden colour and subtle flavour of the saffron as they simmer gently with the tomatoes. I adore the sunny colours of this salad – yellow from the saffron, red from the tomato and green from the basil. Serve this warm, as the heat will release the heady aromas of the basil and saffron.

Saffron Potato Salad with Sun-dried Tomatoes and Caper and Basil Dressing

500 g large waxy yellow-fleshed potatoes, peeled

a pinch of saffron threads, about 20

8 sun-dried tomatoes (the dry kind, not in oil)

caper and basil dressing

6 tablespoons extra virgin olive oil

3 tablespoons chopped fresh basil leaves, plus extra to serve

2 tablespoons salted capers, rinsed and chopped, if large

1–2 tablespoons freshly squeezed lemon juice, to taste

sea salt and freshly ground black pepper

Serves 4

Cut the potatoes into large chunks. Put in a saucepan, add enough cold water to just cover them, then add the saffron and sun-dried tomatoes. Bring slowly to the boil, then turn down the heat, cover and simmer very gently for about 12 minutes until just tender. If the water boils too fast, the potatoes will start to disintegrate. Drain well.

Pick out the now plumped up sun-dried tomatoes and slice them thinly. Tip the potatoes into a large bowl and add the sliced tomatoes.

To make the dressing, put the oil, chopped basil and capers in a small bowl. Add lemon juice, salt and pepper to taste and mix well. Pour over the hot potatoes, mix gently, then serve hot or warm, scattered with extra basil leaves.

New Potato, Carrot and Leek Salad
with Salsa Lombarda

250 g small new potatoes

4 medium carrots, thickly sliced

2 medium leeks, thickly sliced

salsa lombarda

3 tablespoons salted capers, rinsed and dried

4 whole salted anchovies or 8 anchovy fillets in oil, rinsed

1 whole roasted red pepper, deseeded

1 garlic clove

2 tablespoons chopped fresh parsley

4–6 tablespoons extra virgin olive oil

freshly ground black pepper

Serves 4

Another wonderful cooked salad that can be served hot or cold. I often serve this with a hunk of cheese as a main meal. The Salsa Lombarda is normally served with poached fish, but its piquant robust flavours go particularly well with these root vegetables. The sauce comes from Lombardy in Northern Italy, and is good made with the preserved peppers in oil sold in jars for antipasto. If you have the time, you can roast your own.

To make the salsa lombarda, open out the salted anchovies, if using, and lift out and discard the backbone. Rinse under cold water and pat dry. Put the anchovies, roasted red pepper and garlic in a food processor and pulse in short bursts until chopped but not mushy. Transfer to a bowl and stir in 2–4 tablespoons olive oil, depending on how thick you would like the sauce to be. Stir in the parsley and season with black pepper. Set aside.

Bring a large saucepan of salted water to the boil and add the potatoes. Bring back to the boil and simmer for 5 minutes. Add the carrots and leeks to the pan, bring back to the boil and simmer for a further 7–10 minutes or until all the vegetables are tender.

Carefully pour the contents of the pan into a colander and drain thoroughly. Transfer to a large bowl. Spoon the salsa lombarda over the warm vegetables and toss gently. Serve while still warm.

If you ask for a mixed salad in Italy, this is what you will get. Don't be surprised if the tomatoes are not red and ripe, but hard and green – this is how they are eaten in salads. This salad is eaten to cleanse the palate after a meat or fish course, and that is exactly what it does. Leaving the skins on potatoes and tomatoes is generally not done, but feel free to do so if you prefer. In an Italian trattoria, bottles of oil and vinegar are given to you at the table so you can dress your own salad. The vinegar is usually red wine vinegar; balsamic vinegar is not likely to appear in a trattoria.

Classic Trattoria Salad

350 g waxy potatoes, peeled

175 g fine French beans, trimmed

1 tablespoon extra virgin olive oil, plus extra to serve

50 g black or green olives, stoned

1 small crisp lettuce

2 large ripe tomatoes, quartered (or unripe to be authentic)

3 tablespoons chopped fresh parsley

sea salt and freshly ground black pepper

red wine vinegar, to serve

Serves 4

Bring a large saucepan of salted water to the boil, add the potatoes, bring back to the boil and simmer for about 15 minutes or until tender. Add the French beans to the pan 4 minutes before the potatoes are cooked. Drain and cover with cold water to stop the vegetables cooking further. When cold, drain well.

Remove the beans to a bowl, slice the potatoes thickly and add to the beans. Add the olive oil and olives and toss well.

Wash the lettuce and dry well in a salad spinner or with a clean tea towel. Tear into bite-sized pieces and add to the potatoes along with the tomatoes. Toss lightly. Transfer to a serving bowl and sprinkle with parsley. Serve with bottles of olive oil and vinegar and salt and pepper so the salad can be dressed at the table.

Insalata di Verdure Cotte with Salsa Verde

2 red onions

100 g young carrots

1/2 head of celery

100 g courgettes

200 g baby new potatoes

100 g French beans, trimmed

sea salt and freshly ground
    black pepper

salsa verde

1 teaspoon sea salt

2 garlic cloves, finely chopped

4 anchovy fillets in oil, rinsed
    and finely chopped

3 tablespoons chopped
    fresh parsley

3 tablespoons chopped
    fresh mint leaves

3 tablespoons chopped
    fresh basil leaves

2 tablespoons salted capers,
    rinsed and chopped

150 ml extra virgin olive oil,
    plus extra for drizzling

2 tablespoons freshly squeezed
    lemon juice, or to taste

Serves 4–6

Italians do not eat salads as a main course in general, but this is an exception. It makes a good summer lunch dish to linger over. The cooking water makes a delicious stock for cooking pasta or adding to a pasta sauce.

To make the salsa verde, put the salt and garlic in a mortar and pound with a pestle until creamy. Add the anchovies, fresh herbs, capers, oil and lemon juice, to taste. Season with pepper and stir well. Transfer to a small serving bowl, cover and set aside.

Bring a large saucepan of lightly salted water to the boil. Add the whole onions and simmer for 25 minutes.

Meanwhile, halve the carrots lengthways, divide the celery into sticks and cut each stick in half so that they are the same length as the carrots. Quarter the courgettes lengthways. Add the carrots and potatoes to the pan, bring back to the boil and simmer for a further 10 minutes. Add the celery, courgettes and beans and simmer for a further 6 minutes or until all the vegetables are cooked.

Carefully lift out the vegetables with a slotted spoon. Let drain, then arrange in neat piles on a large platter. Cut the onions into quarters. Season the vegetables with salt and pepper and drizzle with olive oil. Serve with the salsa verde.

This is one of the easiest ways to cook and serve a selection of Mediterranean vegetables for a large number of people. Grilling the vegetables concentrates their flavours, and a touch of aged balsamic vinegar cuts through their sweetness. Don't cut the vegetables too small – this salad should be robust and chunky.

Grilled Mixed Vegetable Salad
with Balsamic Herb Dressing

1 medium courgette

1 medium aubergine

1 large red pepper, halved and deseeded

12 tablespoons extra virgin olive oil

2 small red onions, quartered

150 g cherry tomatoes

2 teaspoons balsamic vinegar

1 garlic clove, crushed

3 tablespoons chopped mixed fresh herbs, such as parsley, basil, marjoram or oregano, plus extra to serve

sea salt and freshly ground black pepper

Serves 4

Cut the courgette, aubergine and the pepper halves into large, bite-sized pieces. Transfer to a large bowl, add 6 tablespoons olive oil and toss well. Season to taste with salt and pepper.

Line a grill pan with foil and spoon in the vegetables. Add the onions and spread out the vegetables in an even layer (don't overcrowd the pan or they will stew). Grill under a preheated hot grill for 4–5 minutes or until the edges of the vegetables start to catch. Stir well, add the tomatoes and grill for a further 5 minutes until the vegetables are browned and cooked but not mushy.

Meanwhile, whisk the remaining olive oil with the balsamic vinegar, garlic and herbs. Pour the dressing over the vegetables, toss lightly and transfer to a serving dish. Cover and set aside for at least 30 minutes to let the flavours infuse. Serve sprinkled with extra herbs. Do not serve this chilled as it would ruin the flavour.

Italian Christmas Salad

1 cauliflower (a green romanesco variety looks good)

2 red peppers, roasted

8 anchovy fillets in oil, rinsed and chopped

4 small gherkins, sliced

1 tablespoon salted capers, rinsed and chopped

125 g mixed black and green olives, stoned

4 tablespoons extra virgin olive oil

1 tablespoon white wine vinegar

sea salt and freshly ground black pepper

Serves 4

This is a typical salad served during the festive season when salad leaves are hard to find and cauliflowers are at their peak. Visit an Italian market at this time, especially in the south, and you will see mountains of cauliflowers. If they are a pretty pale green colour, it is because they don't blanch them when they are growing. You could use the bright green, spiky-looking romanesco cauliflower if you like.

Cut the cauliflower into bite-sized florets. Bring a large saucepan of salted water to the boil, add the cauliflower and cook until tender, 6–8 minutes. Drain and refresh in cold water. When cold, drain well and transfer to a bowl.

Cut the peppers in half and remove the stalks and seeds. Cut the flesh into thick strips and add to the cauliflower along with the anchovies, gherkins, capers and olives. Mix well.

Whisk the oil and vinegar together and season to taste with salt and pepper. Pour over the salad and toss gently. Transfer to a serving dish to serve.

The colours in this salad remind me of a Cardinal's rich red robes in Renaissance paintings. I had a salad like this in the Veneto area with spectacular fresh *radicchio di Treviso*. The sweetness of the beetroot contrasts so well with the bitter red radicchio leaves. Add some potatoes for a more substantial salad, if you like. The chives add a taste of onion as well as some contrasting colour.

Cardinal's Salad

4 tablespoons mayonnaise

1 tablespoon red wine vinegar or raspberry vinegar

2 tablespoons extra virgin olive oil

3 tablespoons chopped fresh chives

1 head of radicchio, shredded

500 g cooked beetroot, thinly sliced

$^1/_2$ cucumber, thinly sliced

a bunch of radishes, quartered

3 eggs, hard-boiled and quartered

freshly ground black pepper

Serves 4

Put the mayonnaise, vinegar and olive oil in a bowl and stir to mix. Stir in half the chives and set aside.

Arrange the shredded radicchio on a serving platter. Add a layer of beetroot and a spoonful of the mayonnaise dressing. Add a layer of cucumber and another spoonful of dressing.

Top with the radishes, then the eggs. Drizzle over the remaining dressing, sprinkle with black pepper and the remaining chives and serve.

Grilled Artichoke Salad with Salted Ricotta, Lemon and Marjoram

8–12 medium purply green
   artichokes with stems,
   heads about 10 cm long
   or 12 whole char-grilled
   artichokes in oil, drained

2¹⁄₂ unwaxed lemons

150 ml extra virgin olive oil

2–3 tablespoons chopped
   fresh marjoram

250 g salted ricotta, pecorino
   or feta cheese, cubed

sea salt and freshly ground
   black pepper

Serves 4

Fresh young artichokes are wonderful cooked in this simple way. They are easy to prepare, but it is worth donning a pair of light rubber gloves while you prepare them to avoid black fingers.

First, prepare the fresh artichokes, if using. Fill a large bowl with water and squeeze in the juice of 1 lemon to acidulate it. Use another ¹⁄₂ lemon to rub the cut portions of the artichoke as you work. Snap off the dark outer leaves, starting at the base. Trim the stalk down to about 5 cm. Trim away the dark green outer layer at the base and peel the fibrous outside of the stalk with a vegetable peeler. Cut about 1 cm off the tip of each artichoke. As they are prepared, put the artichokes in the lemony water until needed – this will stop them discolouring. When ready to cook, drain and cut the artichokes in half lengthways, then brush with 50 ml olive oil.

Heat a stove-top grill pan until smoking. Put the artichokes cut side down on the pan and cook for 3 minutes. Turn them over and cook for a further 2–3 minutes until tender. Transfer to a large bowl.

Grate the zest and squeeze the juice from the remaining lemon. Whisk the remaining olive oil with 2–3 tablespoons lemon juice, the lemon zest and marjoram. Season to taste with salt and pepper and add more lemon juice, if necessary. Pour over the artichokes, toss well to coat, then carefully mix in the cheese. Cover and let the flavours infuse for at least 1 hour before serving.

Warm Lentil, Rocket and Mushroom Salad
with Sun-Blushed Tomatoes

200 g green or brown lentils

1 small onion, halved

1 carrot, halved

1 celery stalk, halved

1 bay leaf

3 garlic cloves, 2 lightly crushed
    but kept whole and
    1 finely chopped

150 ml extra virgin olive oil, plus
    about 1 tablespoon for frying

100 g pancetta (Italian bacon),
    cut into matchsticks

450 g large flat mushrooms
    or fresh porcini, wiped
    and thickly sliced

3 tablespoons red wine vinegar

1/2 teaspoon sugar

12 sun-blushed tomatoes, halved

6 spring onions, white and
    green parts, chopped

300 g rocket

sea salt and freshly ground
    black pepper

Serves 6

This warm salad makes an ideal starter. Lentils are very popular throughout Italy and are a symbol of good luck. Some of the best come from Umbria, in the middle of the country.

Put the lentils, onion, carrot, celery, bay leaf and crushed garlic cloves in a large saucepan. Add enough water to completely cover all the ingredients. Bring to the boil, then turn down the heat and simmer for about 45 minutes or until the lentils are tender but not falling apart and mushy. Drain well. Remove and discard the vegetables, then transfer the lentils to a large serving bowl.

Heat about 1 tablespoon oil in a frying pan, add the pancetta and cook until golden and crisp. Remove the pancetta, drain on kitchen paper and add to the lentils. Return the pan to the heat and add the mushrooms. Fry for 2–3 minutes, then add to the lentils.

Add the chopped garlic to the hot pan, along with a little more oil if necessary, and fry until just beginning to colour. Immediately add the vinegar, scraping up any sticky bits in the pan. Add the sugar and boil until it is dissolved. Stir in the olive oil and heat gently – do not let it boil. Season to taste with salt and pepper.

Add the tomatoes, spring onions and rocket to the lentils and mix well. Pour over the hot dressing and toss lightly but thoroughly. Serve immediately before the salad goes soggy.

Marinated Grilled Aubergine
with Salmoriglio Dressing

2 medium aubergines,
    thinly sliced

about 2 tablespoons extra
    virgin olive oil

sea salt

salmoriglio dressing

2 tablespoons red wine vinegar

1–2 teaspoons sugar

finely grated zest and juice of
    $1/2$ unwaxed lemon

4 tablespoons extra virgin
    olive oil

1 garlic clove, finely chopped

2 tablespoons fresh mint leaves,
    finely chopped, plus extra
    leaves to serve

1 tablespoon salted capers,
    rinsed and chopped

Serves 4

This is one of my favourite cold salads. I make it in large quantities and keep it in the fridge for a quick snack – the aubergine just gets better as it absorbs the lemony dressing. It can be eaten on its own, with fresh ricotta or crumbled feta cheese or served as part of a mixed antipasto.

To make the salmoriglio dressing, put the vinegar and sugar in a bowl and stir until dissolved. Add the lemon zest, juice and olive oil and whisk well. Stir in the garlic, chopped mint and capers and set aside to infuse.

Meanwhile, spread out the aubergine slices in a colander and sprinkle with salt. Let drain for 20 minutes. Rinse well, pat dry with kitchen paper, then brush the aubergine slices with olive oil.

Heat a ridged stove-top grill pan until smoking and brush with oil. Alternatively, preheat an overhead grill to high. Grill the aubergine slices in batches for 2–3 minutes on each side until golden brown and lightly charred. Arrange the slices on a serving platter and spoon the dressing over the top. Cover and set aside for 30 minutes so the aubergines absorb the flavours of the dressing. Sprinkle with extra mint leaves and serve.

Fish & Seafood

Bright red peppers and silvery marinated anchovies make a spectacular display. This salad has all the colours of the Italian flag – red, green and white – brought to life by the sunny egg yolks. Marinated anchovies are different to those canned in oil or salted ones; they are silver in colour and the flesh is white.

Grilled Red Pepper, Anchovy and Crumbled Egg Salad with Caper Dressing

4 medium red peppers, halved and deseeded

50 ml extra virgin olive oil

2 eggs, hard-boiled

185 g marinated anchovies, drained and thinly sliced

caper dressing

100 ml extra virgin olive oil

1 tablespoon white wine vinegar

1 tablespoon salted capers, rinsed and chopped

2 tablespoons chopped fresh parsley

sea salt and freshly ground black pepper

Serves 4

Brush the peppers with olive oil and lay them in a grill pan skin side up. Grill under a preheated hot grill until the skins are blackened all over. Remove from the grill, let cool, then slip off the skins. Slice the pepper flesh into thin strips.

To make the dressing, put the oil, vinegar, capers and parsley in a bowl and whisk well. Season with salt and pepper and set aside.

Cut the eggs in half, remove the yolks and crumble them up with a fork. Finely chop the egg whites.

Arrange the pepper strips like the spokes of a wheel on a serving plate. Arrange the sliced anchovies in the same way over the top of the peppers. Spoon over the caper dressing, then scatter with the egg whites, followed by the yolks. Serve immediately.

The perfect starter, this dish looks good and tastes fabulous. Really fresh free-range eggs will make all the difference to this salad, adding to both the colour and flavour. If you have salted anchovies, make sure you rinse them well or soak them before using, or they could make the dish very salty.

Asparagus and Egg Salad
with Anchovy Dressing

500 g asparagus, trimmed and cut into 4 cm lengths

1 tablespoon extra virgin olive oil

4 free-range eggs, hard-boiled

anchovy dressing

4 tablespoons extra virgin olive oil

4 anchovy fillets in oil, rinsed and drained

1 teaspoon salted capers, rinsed

1 teaspoon balsamic vinegar

freshly ground black pepper

Serves 4

Steam the asparagus for about 12 minutes until tender. Drain, refresh in cold water, then drain again. Transfer to a bowl, add 1 tablespoon olive oil and toss well.

To make the dressing, put the oil, anchovies, capers and balsamic vinegar in a mini-blender and blend until smooth. Season to taste with black pepper.

Arrange the asparagus around the edge of 4 shallow bowls like a nest. Quarter the eggs and arrange them in the centre of the asparagus. Spoon the anchovy dressing over the top and serve the salad immediately.

Crab and Chilli Salad with Rocket

250 g fresh white crabmeat

4 tablespoons extra virgin
olive oil

1 garlic clove, finely chopped

1 red chilli, deseeded and chopped

2 celery sticks, finely chopped

freshly squeezed lemon juice,
to taste

sea salt and freshly ground
black pepper

a handful of rocket, to serve

Serves 4

Crab is a great favourite in Venice where I tasted this salad. The small amount of chilli brings out the sweetness of the crab.

Put the crab in a bowl and fluff up with a fork.

Heat the olive oil in a small saucepan and add the garlic, chilli and celery. Cook over low heat for 2 minutes, then remove from the heat and add lemon juice, to taste. Pour over the crab, stir well, taste and season with salt, pepper and more lemon juice, if necessary. Cover and chill for at least 30 minutes. Serve topped with rocket.

Grilled Courgette, Anchovy and Spring Onion Salad

6 medium courgettes

about 6 tablespoons extra
virgin olive oil

2 tablespoons freshly squeezed
lemon juice

2 tablespoons freshly grated
Parmesan cheese

2 anchovies in oil or salt, rinsed,
drained and finely chopped

4 spring onions, finely chopped

Serves 4

Salted anchovies and Parmesan bring out the sweetness of the courgettes. Cook them over a barbecue for a truly smoky taste.

Heat a ridged stove-top grill pan until hot or light a barbecue and wait for the coals to turn white. Cut the courgettes into long thin slices, brush with a little olive oil and grill for 2–3 minutes on each side. Transfer to a serving platter.

Whisk 4 tablespoons oil, the lemon juice, Parmesan and anchovies together and spoon over the courgettes. Sprinkle with the spring onion, cover and let marinate in the refrigerator for 2 hours. Remove from the refrigerator 10 minutes before serving.

Insalata Nizzarda

8 tablespoons extra virgin
    olive oil

3 tablespoons vinegar

2 garlic cloves, crushed

3 tablespoons chopped fresh
    basil leaves, plus extra to serve

3 ripe tomatoes

2 green or yellow peppers,
    deseeded and sliced

1 cucumber, cut into chunks

1 red onion, finely chopped

1 celery stick, sliced

500 g grilled artichokes in oil,
    drained and halved

50 g mixed black and green olives

5–6 radishes, trimmed

250 g best tuna in oil, drained
    and divided into chunks

3 eggs, hard-boiled, quartered

12 anchovy fillets in oil, drained

sea salt and freshly ground
    black pepper

Serves 6

This is one of the few Mediterranean main course salads popular throughout Italy. It originates in Nice (Nizza), which was a part of Italy until 1861. It has many local variations, which means the selection of vegetables may vary but the constants are tomatoes, eggs, olives, tuna and anchovies.

Put the oil, vinegar, garlic and basil in a bowl and whisk. Taste and season well with salt and pepper.

Cut the tomatoes into sixths and put in a large bowl. Add the peppers, cucumber, onion, celery, artichokes, olives and radishes. Spoon over half the dressing and toss well to coat. Pile onto a large serving platter.

Tuck the tuna in the salad and arrange the eggs and anchovies on top. Spoon the remaining dressing over the salad, sprinkle with a few extra basil leaves and serve immediately.

This is a classic combination of ingredients that can't be beaten. It's really worth using dried beans for this as canned beans tend to be a bit mushy. Fresh borlotti beans are even better, they look wonderful – marbled cream and garnet red – and only take 15 minutes to cook. Sadly they lose their fantastic colour after cooking, but they taste deliciously creamy. Red onion brings out the flavour of both the tuna and beans. Jars of quality Italian tuna in oil are the best for this salad – the tuna is light in colour, full of flavour and well worth the expense.

185 g dried borlotti beans, soaked in cold water overnight or 350 g fresh podded beans

6 tablespoons extra virgin olive oil, plus extra for drizzling

1 tablespoon red wine vinegar

3 tablespoons chopped fresh parsley

400 g canned tuna in olive oil, drained and divided into large chunks

2 small red onions, very thinly sliced into rings

sea salt and freshly ground black pepper

Serves 4

Tuna, Borlotti Bean and Red Onion Salad with Parsley Dressing

If using dried beans, drain and rinse the soaked beans. Put in a saucepan and cover with cold water. Bring to the boil, then turn down the heat, cover and simmer for 1–1^1/$_2$ hours or until tender but not falling apart. Drain. If using fresh beans, boil them for about 15 minutes or until tender. Drain. Transfer to a large bowl.

Put the oil, vinegar, parsley and salt and pepper to taste in a small bowl and whisk. Pour over the hot beans and mix. Spoon the bean mixture onto a serving platter, pile the tuna on top, then cover with a tangle of onion slices. Grind plenty of black pepper over the salad, drizzle with extra olive oil and serve.

Mint is used a lot in southern Italy, especially where there has been a Moorish occupation. It is particularly good with fish and vegetables where there is some residual sweetness. In this salad I like to use it as salad leaves and not just as a herb.

Prawn, Chickpea and Mint Salad
with Chilli Dressing

4 tablespoons extra virgin olive oil

500 g uncooked medium prawns, shell on

400 g canned chickpeas, rinsed and drained

1 garlic clove, finely chopped

1 red chilli, deseeded and finely chopped

freshly squeezed lemon juice, to taste

50 g fresh mint leaves
sea salt and freshly ground black pepper

Serves 4

Heat the oil in a frying pan and add the prawns. Stir-fry for 4–6 minutes until they change colour and are cooked through. Tip into a colander placed over a bowl to catch the juices and leave until cold. When cold, peel the prawns, put them in a bowl and add the chickpeas.

Pour the collected juices from the prawns into a small saucepan and add the garlic and chilli. Bring to the boil and boil for 1 minute. Remove from the heat and add lemon juice, salt and pepper to taste. Pour the chilli dressing over the prawns and chickpeas and let cool. Cover and chill in the refrigerator for at least 30 minutes to develop the flavours.

To serve, gently stir the mint leaves into the salad, then pile into 4 serving bowls. Serve immediately, while the mint is still perky.

Versions of this type of salad are found all along the coastal regions of Italy. Use only the freshest seafood, clean it really well and cook it quickly. Use as much lemon as you like to bring out the flavour of the seafood and cut through its richness. Scallops and baby octopus are good additions.

Seafood Salad with Lemon and Parsley

500 g fresh mussels, in the shell

1.5 kg fresh vongole or other small clams, in the shell

250 g small fresh squid, cleaned, tentacles removed and bodies cut into rings

250 g small uncooked prawns, shell on

6 tablespoons extra virgin olive oil

finely grated zest and juice of 1 unwaxed lemon

1 garlic clove, finely chopped

4 tablespoons chopped fresh parsley

1 lettuce, leaves separated

sea salt and freshly ground black pepper

lemon wedges, to serve

Serves 4

Debeard the mussels. Scrub the mussels and clams, discarding any with damaged shells or ones that don't close when sharply tapped. Put them in a large bowl of cold water to purge for about 15 minutes. Drain the mussels and clams and put in a large saucepan. Place the pan over high heat, cover and cook for about 5 minutes, shaking the pan occasionally, until the shells open (discard any that don't open). Tip into a colander placed over a saucepan to catch the juices. Remove the clam and mussel meat from the shells, reserving a few shells to serve, if you like.

Bring the reserved juices to the boil and add the squid and prawns. Cook for 2–3 minutes until opaque. Drain, reserving the juices for freezing and using in a fish stock later, if liked. Peel the prawns. Put the prawns, squid and clam and mussel meat in a bowl and mix.

Put the oil, lemon zest and juice, garlic, salt and pepper in a bowl and whisk. Pour over the seafood, add the parsley and mix well. Cover and chill for at least 1 hour to develop the flavours. Serve the salad really cold, piled onto a bed of lettuce leaves with lemon wedges on the side.

Meat

This is an all-time classic salad, and none the worse for that. The sweet salty Parma ham or a local prosciutto crudo, a yielding soft fruit such as ripe figs and peppery rocket are one of life's perfect combinations. I have been served this with a trickle of aged balsamic vinegar drizzled over the figs, which was amazing. If you find a really aged balsamic vinegar on your travels, buy it, never mind the expense. It will be thick, sweet and syrupy and heaven to use in tiny amounts.

Prosciutto, Fig, Rocket and Parmesan Salad

2 teaspoons good balsamic vinegar

4 tablespoons extra virgin olive oil, plus extra to serve

8 fresh ripe figs (preferably purple ones), quartered

12 thin slices of prosciutto crudo, sliced into strips

200 g rocket

150 g fresh Parmesan cheese

sea salt and freshly ground black pepper

Serves 4

Put the balsamic vinegar, olive oil and salt and pepper to taste in a bowl and whisk well.

Put the figs in a bowl, pour over about 2 tablespoons of the dressing and toss well. Arrange the figs on a serving platter. Put the prosciutto in the bowl, add about 1 tablespoon of the dressing and toss to coat. Arrange on the platter with the figs. Gently toss the rocket with the remaining dressing and add to the platter.

Using a vegetable peeler, shave the Parmesan over the platter. Grind over plenty of black pepper and drizzle with a little olive oil. Serve immediately.

Bresaola, Mozzarella and Baby Spinach Salad with Black Olive Dressing

200 g baby spinach leaves

12 slices of bresaola

2 balls of buffalo mozzarella,
150 g each, cubed

2 tablespoons finely shredded
fresh basil leaves

black olive dressing

6 tablespoons extra virgin
olive oil

finely grated zest and juice
of 1 unwaxed lemon

3 tablespoons finely chopped,
stoned, Greek-style black
olives (the wrinkly ones)

2 sun-dried tomatoes in oil,
drained and finely chopped

sea salt and freshly ground
black pepper

Serves 4

This salad is a fantastic contrast of flavours, colours and textures. Bresaola is a salt-cured fillet of beef that has been air-dried and is sliced very thinly. It has a wonderful purply-red colour and an intense meaty flavour that is cleverly balanced in this recipe by the creamy, bland mozzarella.

Wash the spinach leaves and dry in a salad spinner or with a clean tea towel. Slice the bresaola into thick strips and put in a large bowl. Add the spinach and mozzarella and toss well. Pile onto a serving dish.

To make the dressing, put the oil, lemon zest, olives and tomatoes in a bowl. Add salt, pepper and lemon juice to taste and whisk well. Spoon the dressing over the salad and scatter with the basil.

Serve immediately before the dressing makes the salad wilt.

This is a simple but very indulgent salad. Make sure the salame is cut very thinly so it will begin to melt into the warm dressing.

Hot Potato Salad with Salame
and Creamy Gorgonzola Sage Dressing

350 g medium potatoes, unpeeled

100 g Gorgonzola cheese, crumbled

100 ml double cream

2 tablespoons chopped fresh sage leaves, plus extra to serve

12 thin slices of Italian salame

sea salt and freshly ground black pepper

Serves 4

Put the potatoes in a large saucepan of lightly salted water, bring to the boil and simmer for about 20 minutes or until tender.

Meanwhile, put the Gorgonzola and cream in a small saucepan and heat gently until the cheese melts and the sauce is smooth. Do not let it boil. Stir in the chopped sage and season with salt and pepper. Cover and keep warm.

Drain the potatoes, slice them thickly and put in a serving dish. Pour over the warm Gorgonzola dressing and scatter the salame on top. Sprinkle with extra sage leaves and serve immediately.

This salad combines some of the earthy flavours used in north-eastern Italy, towards Austria and Slovenia. Pork and ham are particular favourites here, and are often cooked with potatoes and caraway seeds. This is a winter salad, and I like to serve it just warm alongside cooked gammon. I love the contrast of cold and hot, soft and crunchy.

Celery and Potato Salad with Hot Pancetta and Mustard Dressing

250 g potatoes, peeled and
    cut into large chunks

4 tablespoons olive oil

100 g cubed smoked pancetta

1 tablespoon wholegrain mustard

a pinch of caraway seeds

2 tablespoons red wine vinegar

2 tablespoons chopped fresh
    parsley, plus extra to serve

1 medium red onion,
    finely chopped

4 celery sticks, sliced

sea salt and freshly ground
    black pepper

Serves 4

Put the potatoes in a large saucepan of salted water, bring to the boil and simmer very gently for about 12 minutes until just tender. Drain and set aside to steam dry and cool slightly.

Heat the oil in a frying pan and add the pancetta. Cook until sizzling and beginning to brown, 1–2 minutes. Remove the pan from the heat and add the mustard and caraway. Return to the heat and cook for a few minutes more. Add the vinegar to the pan and bring to the boil. Boil for 1 minute to evaporate the vinegar, then remove from the heat and stir in the parsley. Taste and season with salt and pepper.

Put the potatoes, onion and celery in a bowl and mix gently. Pile into a serving dish, spoon the dressing over the top and sprinkle with extra parsley. Serve immediately.

Index

A
anchovies: grilled
    courgette, anchovy
    and spring onion
    salad, 47
    grilled red pepper,
    anchovy and
    crumbled egg salad,
    43
    insalata Nizzarda, 48
    Italian Christmas salad,
    32
artichokes: grilled
    artichoke salad, 36
    insalata Nizzarda, 48
asparagus and egg salad,
    44
aubergines: grilled mixed
    vegetable salad, 31
    marinated grilled
    aubergine, 40

B
beetroot: Cardinal's salad,
    35
bitter lettuce and orange
    salad, 18
borlotti bean, tuna and
    red onion salad, 51
bread and summer
    vegetable salad, 17
bresaola, mozzarella and
    baby spinach salad,
    58
broad beans and
    pecorino, 14

C
Cardinal's salad, 35
carrots: insalata di verdure
    cotte, 28
    new potato, carrot and
    leek salad, 24
cauliflower: Italian
    Christmas salad, 32
celery: celery and potato
    salad, 62

insalata di verdure cotte,
    28
cheese: bresaola,
    mozzarella and baby
    spinach salad, 58
    broad beans and
    pecorino, 14
    grilled artichoke salad
    with salted ricotta,
    36
    hot potato salad with
    salame, 61
    prosciutto, fig, rocket
    and Parmesan salad,
    57
    tomato, mozzarella and
    basil salad, 9
chickpea, prawn and mint
    salad, 52
chillies: crab and chilli
    salad, 47
    prawn, chickpea and
    mint salad, 52
clams: seafood salad, 55
classic trattoria salad, 27
courgettes: grilled
    courgette, anchovy
    and spring onion
    salad, 47
    grilled mixed vegetable
    salad, 31
    insalata di verdure cotte,
    28
crab and chilli salad with
    rocket, 47
cucumber: grated
    cucumber, soured
    cream and paprika
    salad, 10
    insalata Nizzarda, 48
    tomato, cucumber and
    onion salad, 13

E
eggs: asparagus and egg
    salad, 44
    grilled red pepper,

anchovy and
    crumbled egg salad,
    43

F
fig, prosciutto, rocket and
    Parmesan salad, 57
French beans: classic
    trattoria salad, 27
    insalata di verdure cotte,
    28

I
insalata Caprese, 9
insalata di verdure cotte,
    28
insalata Nizzarda, 48
Italian Christmas salad, 32

L
leeks: new potato, carrot
    and leek salad, 24
lentil, rocket and
    mushroom salad, 39
lettuce: orange and bitter
    lettuce salad, 18
    simple mixed leaf salad,
    13

M
mushrooms: mushroom
    and rocket salad, 21
    warm lentil, rocket and
    mushroom salad, 39
mussels: seafood salad, 55

O
olives: Italian Christmas
    salad, 32
onions: insalata di verdure
    cotte, 28
    tomato, cucumber and
    onion salad, 13
    tuna, borlotti bean and
    red onion salad, 51
orange and bitter lettuce
    salad, 18

P
pancetta: celery and
    potato salad with hot
    pancetta, 62
    warm lentil, rocket and
    mushroom salad, 39
peppers: grilled mixed
    vegetable salad, 31
    grilled red pepper,
    anchovy and
    crumbled egg salad,
    43
    insalata Nizzarda, 48
    Italian Christmas salad,
    32
potatoes: celery and
    potato salad with hot
    pancetta, 62
    classic trattoria salad, 27
    hot potato salad with
    salame, 61
    insalata di verdure cotte,
    28
    new potato, carrot and
    leek salad, 24
    saffron potato salad
    with sun-dried
    tomatoes, 23
prawns: prawn, chickpea
    and mint salad, 52
    seafood salad, 55
prosciutto, fig, rocket and
    Parmesan salad, 57

R
radicchio: Cardinal's salad,
    35
ricotta: grilled artichoke
    salad with salted
    ricotta, lemon and
    marjoram, 36
rocket: crab and chilli
    salad with rocket, 47
    mushroom and rocket
    salad, 21
    prosciutto, fig, rocket
    and Parmesan salad, 57

warm lentil, rocket and
    mushroom salad, 39

S
saffron potato salad with
    sun-dried tomatoes,
    23
salad leaves: simple mixed
    leaf salad, 13
seafood salad, 55
simple mixed leaf salad,
    13
spinach: bresaola,
    mozzarella and baby
    spinach salad, 58
spring onions: grilled
    courgette, anchovy
    and spring onion
    salad, 47
squid: seafood salad, 55

T
tomatoes: grilled mixed
    vegetable salad, 31
    insalata Nizzarda, 48
    orange and bitter
    lettuce salad, 18
    saffron potato salad
    with sun-dried
    tomatoes, 23
    tomato, cucumber and
    onion salad, 13
    tomato, mozzarella and
    basil salad, 9
    Tuscan bread and
    summer vegetable
    salad, 17
    warm lentil, rocket and
    mushroom salad with
    sun-blushed
    tomatoes, 39
trattoria salad, 27
tuna: insalata Nizzarda, 48
    tuna, borlotti bean and
    red onion salad, 51
Tuscan bread and summer
    vegetable salad, 17